The Man Who Sat in the Park

Story by
Louise Schofield

Illustrations by
Suzie Byrne

Rigby PM Plus Chapter Books
part of the Rigby PM Program
Ruby Level

U.S. edition © 2003 Rigby Education
A division of Reed Elsevier Inc.
1000 Hart Road
Barrington, IL 60010 - 2627
www.rigby.com

Text © 2003 Thomson Learning Australia
Illustrations © 2003 Thomson Learning Australia
Originally published in Australia by Thomson Learning Australia

10 9 8 7 6 5 4 3 2 1
07 06 05 04 03

The Man Who Sat in the Park
   ISBN   0 75786 896 7

Printed in China by Midas Printing (Asia) Ltd

An excerpt from the journal of Bradley Thompson

Contents

CHAPTER 1

Thursday, October 14

School was the usual. At lunchtime I played basketball with Tim and Michael. Michael won our game of H-O-R-S-E.

I walked home with Ben and Shelley. When we passed the park, there was a funny-looking man sitting on our favorite bench under the trees. He was eating baked beans with a plastic spoon, right out of the can.

Ben and I told Mom about him when we got home. She told us to be careful when we go there to play and not to bother him.

CHAPTER 2

Friday, October 15

That man was in the park after school again. He was sitting on OUR bench again. Ben and I put our stuff onto a different bench, but it wasn't the same.

Anyway, Ben wanted to show-off how far he could throw the ball. He thought he could throw it twice as far as me and chucked it high over my head. Ben didn't throw it nearly far enough though, and it landed near the man.

The man threw it back to me.

That man is really strange. His clothes look big and funny, and his beard is the bushiest I've ever seen. And all the time he just sits and watches everyone in the park. It's like he has nothing better to do.

Just before Ben and I left to go home, we saw him get off the bench and walk away. He was kind of shuffling along, as if his legs weren't good. I wonder where he lives.

CHAPTER 3

Saturday, October 16

I went shopping with Dad this morning and got some new shoes and a pencil-case with a special pocket. The zipper on my other one is broken.

Afterward, Mom, Dad, and Ben and I went to the park for some games and a picnic. Shelley and Michael were there too. Later, as Mom was getting out the food, a white van pulled into the parking area and that strange man got out. There were some other men in the van too, but they stayed inside.

We told Mom that he was the man who sat on our bench.

We watched as the man shuffled over. So did the driver of the van, who waved to him when he sat down. Then he drove off.

Mom said the van was from the men's shelter. The man was probably staying there because he didn't have a home. She said Nanna sometimes helped to cook and serve the meals there.

Later, Mom offered the man a slice of chocolate cake. I went with her. He said thank you in a funny sort of way, and I thought he was going to cry.

I told him not to be sad — he was sitting on the best bench in the park. It used to be Ben's and my bench, I said, but we didn't mind if he sat on it sometimes. Then he laughed and ate the cake. He said it was very good cake. Mom and I went back to the others.

When we packed up to go home, the man waved good-bye.

CHAPTER 4

Sunday, October 17

This morning Mom called Nanna. She asked if Ben and I could help out at the men's shelter one day, to see what it was like. Nanna said today would be a good day.

Ben told Mom he didn't want to go. He said he didn't want to cook lunch for a bunch of strangers.

I said I'd go. Maybe the man from the park would be there. I was curious to see what a homeless shelter was like and how many people would be there.

Nanna picked me up in her car. When we arrived at the shelter, there were other helpers there, too. Some of them were Nanna's friends. We all put on aprons and caps, and then washed our hands.

I helped chop the vegetables for a big pot of soup.

At 12 o'clock, a whole lot of men came in for lunch. Nanna served up the soup, and I helped hand out the rolls. Some of the men were stranger than the man from the park, and there were a few who were rude. But most of them seemed nice. The soup was delicious, they said. They asked if I'd helped cook it!

I was surprised to see some boys not much older than me coming in for lunch, too. I don't know why they were there. Nanna said people were homeless for lots of different reasons.

Just when I thought he wasn't coming, I saw the man from the park shuffle in. He saw me, too.

After the man sat down to eat his soup, Nanna told me she knew him a little bit. He was a nice man, she said, but he was lonely. He was from another country where there had been a big war. Once he'd had a home and a family, but now he had nothing.

When lunch was over, the man came over to say hello. He asked me my name and then told me his. It was Stanislav (Nanna told me how to spell it!). He said I could call him Stan.

Nanna and I helped to clean up before we went home.

CHAPTER 5

Monday, October 18

It was really windy today. After school, Ben and I took our kites to the park while Mom took Scraps for a walk. Stan was sitting on his bench, and we waved to him. He seemed to be calling me over.

Mom said I could talk to him for just a minute.

Stan didn't look too good today. I think he was sick. But he had something for me — a paper boat he had made. It was the best one I'd ever seen. He told me to put it on the pond, or that's what I think he was telling me. Stan doesn't speak English too well.

I said thanks, and he smiled.

Anyway, I ran down to the pond to try out the boat. It blew all the way to the other side. I could see Stan laughing, and I waved and shouted that it was the best paper boat anyone had ever made.

Then Mom called me to go home. I had homework to do.

Stan was still waving from his bench when we got to the park gate. I couldn't stop thinking about him as we walked home.

CHAPTER 6

Tuesday, October 19

Stan wasn't there after school today. Ben and I kept on looking over at his bench, expecting him to arrive at any minute. But he didn't come.

Soon Michael and Shelley came and we had a game of tag.

When we got home, I told Mom that Stan wasn't there. She said that she knew already. Nanna had phoned and told her that Stan had been taken to the hospital. She said he wouldn't be visiting the park again for a long time.

CHAPTER 7

Wednesday, October 20

After school, we went to the hospital. Nanna told us where Stan's room was. Mom said maybe we could do something to help. We don't know Stan very well, but he seems to have no-one else.

We took a basket of fruit, and I had a paper plane I'd made for him.

But the lady at the desk said Stan was too sick to see visitors except for close relatives.

I said I didn't think he had any family. She smiled and said she would take the fruit up to him — and the paper plane was the best she'd ever seen.

I said it was for Stan. He would know it was from me.

CHAPTER 8

Thursday, October 21

The park seemed different without Stan sitting on the bench, watching the ducks every day. I played with Ben, but when the ball went too high over my head Stan wasn't there to throw it back.

I told Mom I didn't want to go to the park any more. It only made me think of how sick Stan had looked that last day we'd seen him. And how lonely he had been. I asked if we could call the hospital and find out how he was. Mom said to let it be.

I hope Stan liked my plane.

I think he's going to die.

CHAPTER 9

Friday, October 22

School was horrible today. I just couldn't think, and Mr. Dunston got angry when I didn't hear him ask me a question.

Lunchtime was better. Mom had put an extra big slice of chocolate cake in my lunchbox. And Michael, Tim, and Shelley told me their best jokes to cheer me up.

After school, instead of going to the park, Dad drove us to the beach for a walk. It was windy and the sand flew up behind us.

Scraps got excited and ran all the way to the other end with Ben and me.

Out on the horizon, you could see big gray clouds coming in. It looked like a storm. When we got home, it was raining.

Right now, I can see the park from my bedroom window. Nobody is there. It's empty except for the ducks and swans. They've come up onto the lawn to eat worms.

The rain is clattering on our roof.

This afternoon, for the first time, I noticed that raindrops look like tears when they run down your window.

CHAPTER 10

Sunday, October 24

Yesterday was too wet to do much, so I didn't write. The rain has stopped now.

Nanna came to visit today. She brought along some raffle tickets that her club was selling to raise money. Nanna said the money was going toward the men's shelter, to buy more blankets. I could win a new bike.

I gave her some of my allowance, and she gave me four tickets. She said that she hopes I win. I said that I don't mind if I don't.

When Ben and I walked to Michael's house after lunch, we passed the park gates. I could see Stan's bench, and somebody was there, standing near it.

At first I thought it was Stan, and I was going to run over to say how glad I was that he was better, and ask him if he liked my paper plane. But when I looked again, I saw that it wasn't him. It was the man who drove the van from the men's shelter.

He was holding some flowers, like the ones that grow near the park gate.

On the way home, we passed the park again. The van driver was gone, but the flowers were on the bench where Stan used to sit.

CHAPTER 11

Saturday, November 20

Today's my birthday. I haven't written in my journal for a long time because it was making me sad. But today something special happened. I thought I'd better write again, so I'll always remember it.

When I woke up this morning, I couldn't wait to open my birthday presents. I got a tool kit from Nanna, a box of dinosaurs from Ben, and behind all the other presents was a really big box from Mom and Dad.

Everyone said, "Open the big box! Open the big box!" So I did.

I ripped off the paper and inside there was a fantastic boat with a sail. It was red and blue – the best one I'd ever seen.

I wanted to go to the pond to test it right away. I couldn't wait to get there.

But when I saw the park, I didn't feel happy any more. I remembered the man who used to sit there. I'd been trying not to think too much about Stan.

I think Mom knew how I felt. I could tell by the way she squeezed my hand. Dad said he wondered if my boat would sail all the way to the other side.

I put it in the water and pushed it off.

As the boat sailed away, I looked at the bench where Stan used to sit. I almost expected him to be there watching. It seemed kind of empty without him.

I felt really sad again.

Mom said that even though Stan's not here any more, and we wish he could be, she's sure he wouldn't want me to be sad forever.

As I was thinking about what Mom had said, I felt as though Stan would have been happy watching us. And I felt a little better.

My new boat sailed right across the water. The wind was just right and pushed it all the way to the other side. We all shouted, "Hurray!"

Suddenly I thought of the paper boat that Stan had made for me. Then I knew.

Mom and Dad gave me the sailing boat to have happy memories of Stan – the man who sat in the park.